How to use this book

This book is an identification guide to breeds of horses and ponies from all over the world. Take it with you when you go to shows, riding stables, racetracks or any place that you might see horses.

The breeds are arranged with ponies first, followed by riding horses, harness horses and draught horses.

Next to each picture is a short description of the breed, telling you where the breed comes from, what kind of work it does, the colors it can be, and its height. It also points out any special details about the breed.

Some of the colors have unusual names. You can look them up on page 7. If there are any other words you don't understand, look them up in the glossary on page 58, or find them on the diagram showing the parts of a horse on page 49.

Scorecard

There is a small blank circle next to each description. When you see a breed, put a check in the circle. You will be able to find some of the breeds in this book all over North America. Others live either in particular areas of the country, or in other countries, so they will be harder to find. Others are very rare indeed; you will probably see them only in zoos, or in a film or on television. The scorecard at the end of the book gives a score for each breed you see. A common breed scores 5 points, and a very rare one 25 points.

Height

The height of horses and ponies is measured in hands, from the ground to the top of the withers. One hand equals 4 inches. If the description says that a horse is 15.2 hh, for example, it means that the horse is 15 hands and 2 inches high (hh means "hands high"). Ponies usually grow up to 14.2 hh.

Withers

Height is measured in hands

Check off each horse or pony when you have seen it

How horses began

Arab horse

Exmoor pony

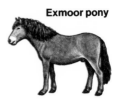

The first horse looked rather like a deer. It lived in forests and woodlands, 50 million years ago. Gradually, different types of horses began to appear. They all became fast and surefooted, because they had to be able to run away from their enemies.

All the breeds we know today are descended from two ancient types of horses – the southern type, from the hot deserts of North Africa and southern Asia, and the northern type, from cold, hilly or mountainous parts of Europe and Asia.

Wild Horses
The only truly wild breed left in the world is the Przewalski, from the Gobi Desert in Mongolia, where some still live in wild herds.

The southern type had a fine, silky coat and light bones. It could run fast and survive on small amounts of food. It was similar to the Arab horse of today. The northern type had a thick, rough coat and sturdy legs. It lived off poor, scrubby grass and bushes. This type was similar to breeds like the Przewalski and Exmoor of today. Several thousand years ago, in Europe, people began to control the development of horses like these. There are now about 200 different breeds of horses and ponies.

The Przewalski

How horses are used

To begin with, horses were hunted for food. Later on they were bred to do all sorts of work. Harness horses, for example, pull light carts and carriages, while draft horses are used for ploughing and hauling (pulling heavy carts and wagons). Today, people ride mostly for pleasure or sport, although some horses still work on farms, especially in eastern Europe.

Heavy draft horse pulling a plough

In the 19th century, three Arab stallions were crossed with English hunters to produce the Thoroughbred, the finest riding horse ever bred. It gets its qualities of speed, good looks and endurance from the Arab.

Thoroughbred racehorses

Looking at horses

At first, it is difficult to tell what breed a horse or pony is, but after a while, it becomes easier. Here are some clues to help you:

Welsh pony

Highland pony

If the horse carries its tail high and has a dished profile (a face that curves in), it probably has some Arab blood. It may be an Anglo-Arab, or even a Welsh pony.

If it is small and sturdy, with a long, rough coat, it is probably a mountain or moorland pony – perhaps a Highland or Dartmoor pony.

Thoroughbred

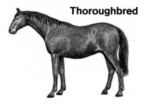

Percheron

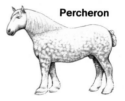

If the horse is tall, with long legs, a fine skin and coat, and a light build, it is probably a Thoroughbred.

If it is big, heavy and slow, with feather (long hairs) around its fetlocks, it is probably a draft horse, like a Percheron or a Shire.

Where to look

Many of the horses you see are likely to be cross-bred. It can be fun trying to guess which different breeds their ancestors were. Look for pure-bred horses and ponies at:

Horse shows, where there are classes for various breeds.

Stud farms, where horses are bred. (This is probably the best place to find pure breeds.)

The breed's natural surroundings such as the marshes on Assateague Island (Virginia), the Rocky Mountains and the Great Plains.

Racing stables or racetracks (these are the best places to see Thoroughbreds).

Riding stables. At the Spanish Riding School in Vienna, for example, you will see only Lipizzaners.

Ask at your nearest riding school if any of their horses or ponies are pure-bred.

Colors and markings

Most breeds are the common colors—bay, brown, chestnut, and gray. Some are generally a particular color. For example, the Fjord pony is usually dun.

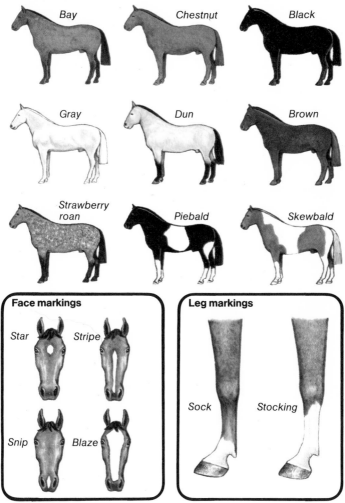

Bay

Chestnut

Black

Gray

Dun

Brown

Strawberry roan

Piebald

Skewbald

Face markings

Star

Stripe

Snip

Blaze

Leg markings

Sock

Stocking

Ponies

Thick mane
and tail

Highland ▶
Comes from the Scottish
Highlands. Largest British
pony. Once used as a
pack pony. Popular for
driving and riding.
Usually gray or dun; can
be black or
chestnut. Long
winter coat.
Up to 14.2 hh.

Short, strong
neck

◀ Shetland
Smallest British pony.
Once used to carry peat.
Popular as pet for riding
and driving. Usually black,
brown or chestnut. Can be
piebald or
skewbald.
About 9.2 hh.

Dales ▶

Comes from the Pennine
hills, in northern England.
Was used as a pack pony;
now used in harness and
on farms. Slightly bigger
and heavier than the Fell
pony. Usually dark brown
or black. May
have white
markings.
Up to 14 hh.

Lots of
feather

◀ Fell

Comes from higher
regions of the western
Pennines. Still used by
farmers for herding
cattle and sheep.
Usually black,
sometimes brown or
bay. No white
markings.
About 14 hh.

Light-colored
muzzle

Rough,
springy
coat

Exmoor ▶
Oldest breed in Britain.
Several herds still live half-
wild on Exmoor, in
southwest England. Hardy
and strong willed. Good
riding ponies for children.
Bay or brown with
light-colored
underside.
Up to 12.3 hh.

Small, pretty
head

◀ Dartmoor
Lives half-wild on
Dartmoor, southwest
England. Hardy and sure-
footed. Excellent
children's riding pony.
Intelligent and elegant.
Bay, black or
brown. Up to
12.2 hh.

New Forest ▶
Lives in the New Forest, in
southern England. Very
hardy. Good riding pony.
Can be various shapes.
Any color except
piebald or
skewbald.
12-14 hh.

Long neck

◀ Connemara
Comes from northwest
Ireland. Ancestors were
probably Spanish and
Arab horses. Fast and
surefooted. Jumps well.
Usually gray; also dun,
black, brown, bay
and chestnut.
13-14 hh.

11

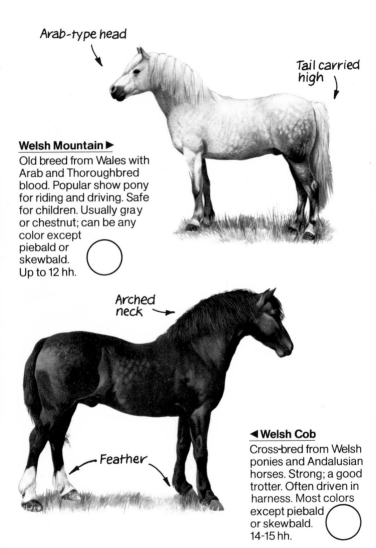

Arab-type head

Tail carried high

Welsh Mountain ▶
Old breed from Wales with Arab and Thoroughbred blood. Popular show pony for riding and driving. Safe for children. Usually gray or chestnut; can be any color except piebald or skewbald. Up to 12 hh.

Arched neck

Feather

◀ Welsh Cob
Cross-bred from Welsh ponies and Andalusian horses. Strong; a good trotter. Often driven in harness. Most colors except piebald or skewbald. 14-15 hh.

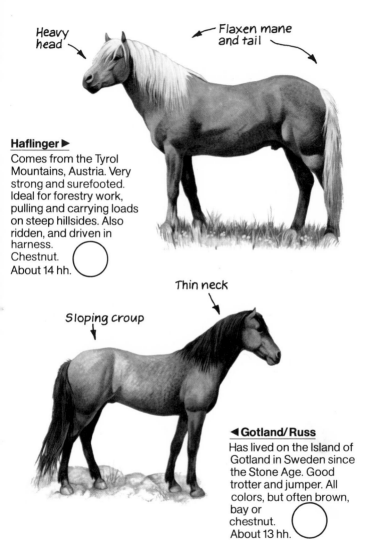

Heavy head →

← Flaxen mane and tail →

Haflinger ▶
Comes from the Tyrol Mountains, Austria. Very strong and surefooted. Ideal for forestry work, pulling and carrying loads on steep hillsides. Also ridden, and driven in harness.
Chestnut.
About 14 hh.

Thin neck ↓

Sloping croup ↓

◀ Gotland/Russ
Has lived on the Island of Gotland in Sweden since the Stone Age. Good trotter and jumper. All colors, but often brown, bay or chestnut.
About 13 hh.

13

Icelandic ▶
Bred from various northern European ponies. Used as riding or pack pony. Some are bred to eat. Quiet and friendly. Any color; often gray, dun brown, black or chestnut.
12-13 hh.

High knee action ◀—

Mane cut in crest like shape ↘

◀ Fjord
Comes from Norway. Good all round worker – used for riding, driving, hauling and carrying. Yellow dun, with black and silver mane and tail.
13-14.2 hh.

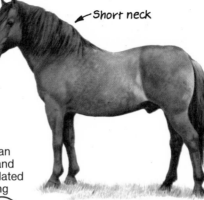

← Short neck

Huçul▶

Comes from Carpathian Mountains of Russia and Rumania. Probably related to Tarpan breed. Strong pack pony. Brown, dun or bay.
About 13 hh.

◀Kazakh

Comes from Russia. Good long distance racing pony. Mares' milk used to make a fermented drink called "kumis". Any color; often bay, brown or chestnut.
About 13 hh.

15

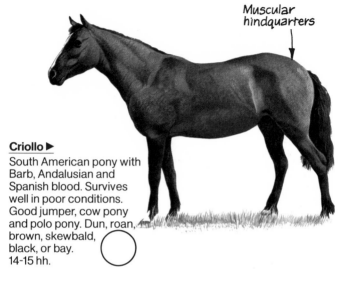

Muscular
hindquarters

Criollo ▶

South American pony with
Barb, Andalusian and
Spanish blood. Survives
well in poor conditions.
Good jumper, cow pony
and polo pony. Dun, roan,
brown, skewbald,
black, or bay.
14-15 hh.

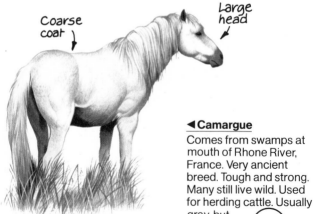

Coarse
coat

Large
head

◀ Camargue

Comes from swamps at
mouth of Rhone River,
France. Very ancient
breed. Tough and strong.
Many still live wild. Used
for herding cattle. Usually
gray, but
born brown.
14-15 hh.

Long, silky coat

Falabella ▶
Comes from Argentina.
A miniature horse;
not very strong. Good
natured; popular
children's pet and
driving pony.
Any color
Less than 7 hh.

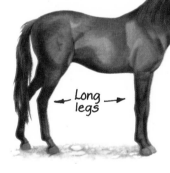

Long
legs

◄ Caspian
Wild pony from Iran. Only
about 100 still exist.
Shaped like a miniature
Thoroughbred. Good at
jumping. Usually bay or
brown; also gray. Never
has white
markings.
9.2-11.2 hh.

17

Coarse mane and coat

Tarpan ▶
Oldest breed in Europe
and northern Asia. Was
once hunted for food. Two
wild herds live in forests in
Poland. Very hardy.
Usually light brown with
black ears, mane,
tail, and legs.
About 13 hh.

Upright mane

Large head

Thin
tail

◀ Przewalski
Also called Asiatic or
Mongolian Wild Horse.
Unchanged since the Ice
Age. Only about 300 exist,
some in zoos, others in
herds in Gobi Desert,
Mongolia. Bay or
dun color.
12-14 hh.

Dark
muzzle

Rounded
body

Pony of the Americas ▶
New breed from the United
States. Good children's
riding pony. Spotted
coloring, similar
to the
Appaloosa.
11.2-13.2 hh.

◀ Sable Island Pony
Comes from Nova Scotia,
Canada. Small and rough.
Lives in wild herds. Feeds
off scrub grass on sand
dunes. Some are sold for
children to ride. All
colors, but often
chestnut.
About 14 hh.

19

Riding Horses

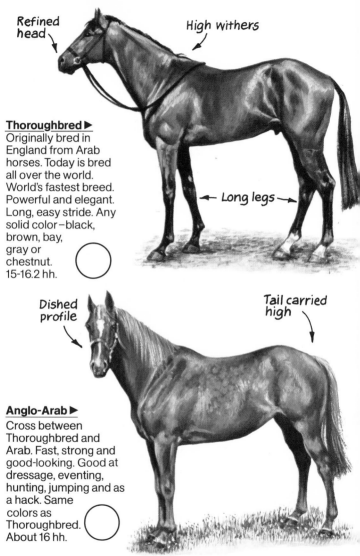

Refined head

High withers

Thoroughbred ▶
Originally bred in England from Arab horses. Today is bred all over the world. World's fastest breed. Powerful and elegant. Long, easy stride. Any solid color – black, brown, bay, gray or chestnut. 15-16.2 hh.

Long legs

Dished profile

Tail carried high

Anglo-Arab ▶
Cross between Thoroughbred and Arab. Fast, strong and good-looking. Good at dressage, eventing, hunting, jumping and as a hack. Same colors as Thoroughbred. About 16 hh.

High tail

American Saddlebred ▶
Once used by families in the South of the United States as a riding and harness horse. Has three to five ambling gaits (paces). Smooth, effortless ride. Bay, brown, or chestnut. 15-15.3 hh.

High knee action

Pinkish muzzle

◀ Appaloosa
North American Indian horse. Cow pony, hunter and jumper. Three main color types – dark pinkish with lighter back and black spots on loins and hips; white with black spots; bay or black with white spots on hips and loins. 14-15.3 hh.

Hooves are striped

Head nods
with each
step

◄ Tennessee Walking Horse
From Tennessee and Louisiana. Has three special gaits –flat-footed walk; running walk; and running canter. Trots only in harness. Used for riding, driving and farm work. All solid colors.
15.2-16 hh.

Long pasterns

Thick tail

Morgan ►
Originally bred from Justin Morgan, a New England stallion. Solid and well muscled. Bay, brown, black or chestnut.
14-15.1 hh.

Deep, elegant body

Powerful
hindquarters

Quarter Horse ▶
Comes from the
United States.
Named after quarter
mile races. Used on
ranches as a cow
pony and at rodeos.
Many make excellent
hunters and jumpers.
Quick and intelligent.
Any
color.
15-16 hh.

Short
neck

Sloping
croup

◀ Paso Fino
American breed
descended from
horses of Spanish
explorers. Has five
extra gaits. Doesn't
trot. Some do
special, slow "paso
fino" gait.
Any color.
13-15.2 hh.

Thick, arched neck →

Straight profile

◄ Andalusian
Comes from Jerez region of Spain. Ancestors were Barb and Arab horses and native ponies. Very surefooted. Popular riding horse. Gray, black, bay or brown. 15.2-16 hh.

Special tack for bullring

Lusitano ▶
Portuguese horse with same ancestry as Andalusian. Used by army; on farms; and in bull rings. Slightly taller and lighter build than Andalusian. Gray, brown or bay. 15-16 hh.

Small, fine head with dished profile ➤

Tail carried high ↘

Shagya Arab ▶
A type of Arab from eastern Europe. Can live on little or poor food. Tireless. Popular as a cavalry horse in World War I. Usually gray.
14-15 hh.

Large eyes

Longish back

◀ Polish Arab
Another type of Arab. Bred in Poland since 1500. Used as a racehorse. Very tough and strong. Many exported to North America. Can be bay, gray or chestnut.
14.2-15.1 hh.

Long neck

Budyonny ▶
From Rostov in Russia.
Can live on poor food.
Once used as a cavalry
horse. Now used for
dressage, racing and
long distance riding.
Brown, black,
bay or chestnut.
About 16 hh.

Upright shoulders

Don ▶
Comes from Don
Valley, Russia.
Once ridden by the
Cossacks. Survives well
in poor grasslands.
Often used as a
carriage horse. Short,
jerky stride.
Always
chestnut.
15-16 hh.

Long
legs

High, narrow body

Akhal-Teke ▶
Ancient breed from Turkoman Steppes, Russia. Used for jumping, racing, dressage and long-distance riding. Can stand great heat or cold. Golden chestnut, bay, black or gray.
About 15.1 hh.

Fine coat with metallic sheen

Fine, thin tail

◀ Karabair
Comes from the mountains of central Asia. Can work in dry, hot weather. Fast and good natured. Gray, bay or chestnut. 14.2-15.2 hh.

White mane and tail

Often has white face markings

◄ Palomino
Popular in the United States. Descended from Arab horses. Classed either as a breed or a color. Most are bred for shows. Some jump and hunt. Color varies from cream or light blond to chestnut. 14-16 hh.

An Overo may have a white head

Overo marking type

Pinto ►
Bred in the United States. Used for riding and herding. Two marking types: overo – white areas begin on underside and extend upward in an irregular pattern; tobiano – white starts on back and spreads downward usually in a regular pattern.
Various heights.

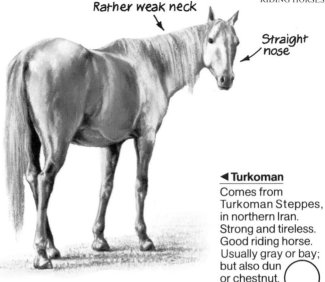

Rather weak neck

Straight nose

◄ Turkoman
Comes from
Turkoman Steppes,
in northern Iran.
Strong and tireless.
Good riding horse.
Usually gray or bay;
but also dun
or chestnut.
14.3-15.2 hh.

Sloping shoulders

Trakehner ►
Bred mainly in
Poland and
Germany. Works as
a farm and cavalry
horse. Gentle but
brave. Good at
jumping and
dressage. Can be
bay, brown,
black or
chestnut.
16-16.2 hh.

Ram-shaped head

Anglo Norman ▶

Cross-bred in England from big war horses brought over by William the Conqueror. Brave and strong. Good riding and jumping horse. Often chestnut. 15.2-16.3 hh.

Lots of feather

◀ Gudbrandsaal

Also called Ostland Horse or Dølehest. Comes from Norway. Strong, medium sized horse, once used for pack work. Usually black, brown or bay. About 15 hh.

Strong
hindquarters

Heavy
shoulders

◄ Hanoverian
German breed
descended from
war horses ridden in
Middle Ages. Strong.
Good show jumper.
Any solid color;
often bay
or brown.
16-17 hh.

Holstein ►
Bred in marshes of
River Elbe, West
Germany. Big and
strong. Good
carriage horse and
show jumper.
Usually brown,
bay or
black.
16-16.2 hh.

31

Knabstrup ▶

Danish breed descended from a spotted Spanish mare. Popular as a circus horse. Fast and hardy. Always spotted. Usually white with black spots. About 15 hh.

Short, arched neck

Lipizzaner ▶

Austria's famous breed, used by the Spanish Riding School in Vienna. Bred from Andalusian horses. Excellent dressage horse; also good in harness. Born brown or black, changes to gray. Pure white in old age. 14.3-16 hh.

32

Barb ▶
Comes from North Africa. There are few pure-bred Barbs left. Can live on poor feed. Fast over short courses. Usually bay, gray, black, brown or chestnut. 14-15 hh.

Hard legs and feet

Narrow hindquarters

High withers

◀ Waler
First bred in New South Wales, Australia. Former cavalry horse, now herds cattle on ranches. Also used at rodeos, for show jumping and general riding. Any solid color. 15-16 hh.

Harness Horses

◄ Standardbred
Famous trotting
horse from the
United States. It had
to reach a standard
speed to become
registered, hence
the name. Races in
carts called sulkies.
Any solid color;
usually bay,
black, or
brown.
15-16 hh.

Long back

Orlov Trotter ►
Comes from Russia,
and is named after
Count Orlov. Strong
and quite heavy;
once used by
cavalry. Fairly high
knee action. Often
gray, also
black or bay.
15.2-17 hh.

Some
feather

Thick, curly mane and tail →

Feather →

◄ Friesian
From Friesland, in the Netherlands. Bred in the Middle Ages to carry knights in armor. Works mostly in harness. Strong and kindly. Always black. About 15 hh.

Tail carried high →

Gelderlander ►
Comes from Gelderland, in the Netherlands. Once worked on farms. Now used for riding and in harness. Chestnut, gray, bay or brown. 15.2-16 hh.

Wide body

Ram-shaped nose

◄ Groningen
Farm horse from the
Netherlands. Heavy
but fast. Can live on
poor food. Good in
harness or for riding.
Usually black,
bay or
brown.
15.2-16 hh.

Heavy neck

◄ Oldenburger
From northwest
Germany. Big and
strong; fairly fast.
Good trotting and
carriage horse.
Usually gray, bay,
black or
brown.
16.2-17.2 hh.

Sloping shoulders

Cleveland Bay ▶
Comes from
Yorkshire, England.
Sure footed, but not
very fast. Used for
carriage work. Good
jumper. Always bay,
without
white
markings.
15-16.2 hh.

High tail

Long back

◀ Hackney
English high-stepping
trotter, famous for its
exaggerated but
graceful action. Used
in light carriages,
for showing.
Bay, black
or brown.
14.3-15.3 hh.

Basic type

Kustanair ▶
From Kazakhstan, in Russia. Good all rounder. Three sorts: Steppe – heavy and slow; Riding – light; Basic – between the two (the most popular). Solid colors, usually bay or chestnut. 15-15.2 hh.

Finnish ▶
Works mainly on farms and in forests in Finland. Also used in trotting races and for riding. Gentle and alert. Usually chestnut. Often has white markings. About 15.2 hh.

Frederiksborg ▶
Old breed from
Denmark. Used
on farms and for
riding. Strong, lively
action. Hard worker.
Usually
chestnut.
Up to 16 hh.

← Short legs →

Roman nose

Kladruber ▶
From
Czechoslovakia.
First bred by
Emperor Maximilian II
in 16th century. Used
in teams to pull state
coaches, on farms
and in dressage
competitions.
Black or
gray.
16-17 hh.

Smallish eyes →

Nonius ▶
Comes from Hungary. Named after Anglo-Norman stallion that founded the breed. Works on farms. Black, bay or brown. Two types: small – about 15.2 hh; large – up to 17 hh.

Light type

◀ Wielkopolski
Popular Polish breed. Many types: heavy ones used on farms; light ones to drive or ride. Many bred at state-owned studs. Usually bay, brown or chestnut. About 16 hh.

Draft Horses

Short back

Big, round feet

Clydesdale ▶
Comes from Scotland. Strong and active, but not too heavy. Popular on farms. Bay, brown or black, with white on feet, face, and underside. About 17 hh.

Narrow head

Shire ▶
Great English draft horse. Once carried knights in armor. Pulls wagons and works on farms. Hard worker. Usually bay, black or gray; lots of white markings. Up to 18 hh.

Lots of feather

Thick neck

Wide chest

◄ Suffolk Punch
Short, stocky breed from Suffolk, England. Does well on little or poor food. Very good natured. Always chestnut. About 16 hh.

◄ Irish Draft
Good all round farm horse, from Ireland. Makes a top class hunter and jumper if crossed with a Thoroughbred. Often bay; also gray, chestnut or brown. 15.2-16 hh.

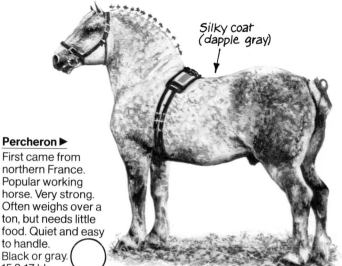

Silky coat
(dapple gray)

Percheron ▶
First came from
northern France.
Popular working
horse. Very strong.
Often weighs over a
ton, but needs little
food. Quiet and easy
to handle.
Black or gray.
15.2-17 hh.

Heavy neck
and shoulders

Ardennes ▶
Ancient breed from
France and Belgium.
Once used by
Napoleon's cavalry.
Powerful and gentle.
Can live out in bad
weather. Usually
roan, bay or
chestnut.
About 15.2 hh.

Short head

Dapple gray colour

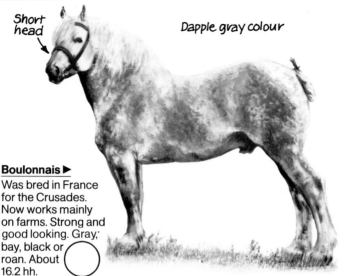

Boulonnais ▶

Was bred in France for the Crusades. Now works mainly on farms. Strong and good looking. Gray, bay, black or roan. About 16.2 hh.

Breton Heavy Draft ▶

Comes from northwest France. Strong, rugged working horse. Related to Postier Breton (carriage horse). Usually strawberry roan, also bay or chestnut. 15-16 hh.

Muscular body

Arched neck

◀ Trait du Nord
Comes from northern France. Breed is being built up; many killed during World War II. Similar to Ardennes. Quiet and gentle. Usually bay, roan or chestnut. About 16 hh.

◀ Auxois
One of the oldest French breeds. Once used for carriage and farm work. Powerful working horse. Usually bay or strawberry roan. Never black or gray. About 15.2 hh.

Heavy neck

Avelignese ▶
Bred mainly in Tuscany, in northern Italy. Once used as a pack pony or light draft horse. Short and muscular. Often long-lived. Usually chestnut. About 14.2 hh.

Very deep body

Jutland ▶
Danish horse once used by the Vikings. Works on farms, and pulls brewers' wagons in Denmark. Often chestnut, but also roan, black, gray, bay, or light brown. 15.2-15.3 hh.

Very short legs

◀Schleswig

Comes from northern Germany. Once used to carry knights in armor. Now used mostly on farms, and for hauling. Nearly always chestnut.
15.2-16 hh.

Short legs

◀Pinzgauer Noriker

Oldest Austrian breed. May be descended from a Roman breed. Quiet and strong. Good for pulling ploughs. Bay, chestnut or spotted.
15-16 hh.

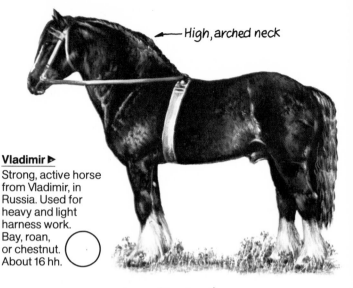

High, arched neck

Vladimir ▶
Strong, active horse
from Vladimir, in
Russia. Used for
heavy and light
harness work.
Bay, roan,
or chestnut.
About 16 hh.

Short neck

Heavy, muscular body

Dutch Draft ▶
Ancient, very pure
breed. Bred from
Belgian horses.
Popular on farms in
the Netherlands,
where it has its own
show. Very strong
and heavy. Bay, gray
or chestnut.
Up to
16.3 hh.

Points of the horse

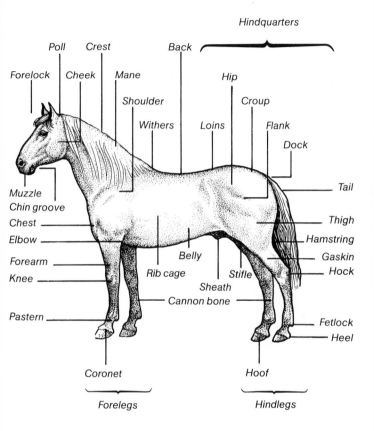

Hindquarters

Poll Crest Back

Forelock Cheek Mane Hip

Shoulder Croup

Withers Loins Flank

Dock

Muzzle

Chin groove

Chest

Elbow

Forearm Belly

Knee Rib cage Stifle

Sheath

Pastern Cannon bone

Coronet Hoof

Forelegs Hindlegs

Tail

Thigh

Hamstring

Gaskin

Hock

Fetlock

Heel

Looking after a pony

Keeping a pony in a field

In the wild, ponies live in herds; they move about a great deal, grazing and drinking, and rest for only a few hours at night. There are many things they may miss in captivity. If you keep your pony in a field, try to give it:

● Other horses or ponies to keep it company.

● Good grazing. Each pony needs at least one acre of good grass. You may need to change fields in spring or fall, to let the grass grow again. Pick up manure to stop worms from spreading.

● Plenty of fresh water to drink.

● Shelter. Trees, a thick hedge or a shed. Keep a salt or mineral block in the shed.

● Strong fencing. A post-and-rail, wood fence is best. Wire is all right if it is tightly fixed to strong posts, with the bottom wire at least 18 inches from the ground.

Thick hedge or shed for shelter

Constant supply of fresh water

Other horses or ponies for company

Strong post-and-rail fence

Keeping a pony in a stable

It isn't natural for ponies to live indoors. If you keep your pony in a stable, it will need special care. You must do the following things:

● Exercise your pony every day. Ride it for at least one hour, or turn it out in a field for a few hours.

● Give it the right kind of food. A pony needs plenty of bulk food, like hay, to nibble during the day and night. It also needs short food, like oats, in small amounts, in the morning, at night, and perhaps at midday.

● Make sure it always has plenty of fresh water.

Stable equipment

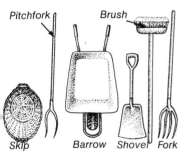

Pitchfork Brush

Skip Barrow Shovel Fork

● Clean out the stable every morning. Clear out wet straw and droppings to stop bad smells and thrush (foot disease). Add fresh bedding of straw, wood shavings, peat or sawdust. The bed must be thick enough to keep the pony warm and keep it from hurting itself. Clean out the manure at night, too.

● Groom your pony every day. This will keep its coat clean and its skin healthy.

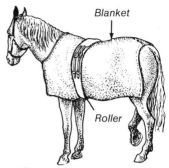

Blanket

Roller

● Keep your pony warm in winter. If it has a full coat, one blanket will do. If it has been clipped, it will need two blankets.

● Let fresh air into the stable to keep your pony from getting coughs and colds. Leave the top door open unless it is bitterly cold. To avoid drafts, it is best if the window and door are on the same side of the stable.

If you want to change your pony's feeding or exercise pattern, do it gradually. Ponies need time to get used to new routines.

Leave top door open

Feeding

What a pony eats

In its natural environment, a pony eats small amounts of bulk food (mostly grass) almost nonstop throughout the day. A pony kept in a stable eats hay instead of grass. The best type of hay to feed your pony is meadow or mixture hay.

If you keep your pony in a field, it may need no extra food during the summer, providing there is plenty of good grass; but watch that it doesn't overeat.

During the winter, when the grass has stopped growing and is very poor, your pony may need up to 12 pounds of hay a day, and even more in frosty or snowy weather.

As well as grass or hay, a pony may need high protein "short" feeds. These are a mixture of corn or cubes and a bulk food like bran or chaff.

You can use these foods to make up a short feed for your pony:

● Corn – Oats or barley. Use crushed or split oats rather than whole oats. Barley is more fattening but has less food value than oats. Use either crushed barley, or whole barley boiled for two to three hours.

● Cubes – Animal food firms sell different kinds of cubes (also called "nuts"). Read the feeding instructions on the sack carefully.

● Bran – Mix bran into a feed with corn or cubes. It will make your pony eat more slowly and digest its food better.

● Chaff – Chopped hay. Use chaff in the same way as bran.

● Flaked maize – A rich and rather fattening food, unsuitable for small ponies.

● Sugar beet – Good for fattening ponies up. Soak it in water for 24 hours before feeding.

● Linseed – Occasionally give your pony small amounts of boiled linseed; it has good food value and will improve your pony's coat.

● Vegetables – If there is no grass, give your pony fresh root vegetables, or green leaves like sprouts or cabbage leaves. Chop carrots, mangolds, turnips and parsnips lengthwise before adding them to the feed.

Remember to leave a salt or mineral lick (block) in your pony's field or stable.

Haynet ➤

▲ **Put hay in a rack or haynet to prevent it being wasted.**

If it is likely to rain, feed the pony inside its stable

Bin

▲ **Put short feeds in a manger or galvanized bin.**

How to feed a pony

These are the basic rules for feeding a pony:

- Make sure your pony always has enough grass or hay to eat.
- Feed your pony little and often. Ponies have small stomachs, so they can't digest large meals properly.
- Give your pony water to drink before you feed it, not afterwards.
- Never ride your pony straight after a feed; wait about an hour.
- Feed your pony at the same time every day.

Each pony will need different amounts of different kinds of food. What you feed your pony will depend on its temperament, size and health, how much work it has to do, the time of year, where the pony is kept, how much good grass is available, and how much the pony has to eat to keep its weight up.

The table below will give you an idea of what you might feed an average 14 hh pony in one day, at different times of the year.

Table showing approximate daily feeds for an average 14 hh pony				
SEASON	Summer	Summer	Winter	Winter
WHERE KEPT	Field	Field	Stable	Stable
WORK	Light riding	Daily training and shows	Light riding	Daily exercise and hunting
EARLY MORNING		2lb hay, 2lb cubes (if the pony is worked very hard)	6lb hay	4lb hay 1lb oats, 1lb cubes, 1lb bran or chaff dampened with water
MID-DAY				4lb hay, 1lb oats, 1lb cubes, 1lb bran or chaff dampened with water
EVENING	1-2lb cubes (if there is too little good grass)	2lb hay 2lb oats, 1lb bran or chaff dampened with water	4lb hay, 2-3lb oats, 1lb bran or chaff ½lb sugar beet (weigh before soaking), 1-2lb fresh vegetables	4lb hay, 1lb oats, ½lb flaked maize, ½lb sugar beet (weigh before soaking), 1-2lb fresh vegetables

Grooming

You must groom your pony every day if it is kept in a stable.

Pick out its feet with a hoof pick, pulling the pick from heel to toe.

If your pony has a full coat, take off dirt and stains with a dandy brush, working back from the top of its neck. Always brush in the direction the coat lies.

Next, clean its skin and coat with the body brush. This brush has short, soft hairs. Clean the brush by pulling it across a metal or rubber currycomb. Brush the pony's head with the body brush, too, taking care not to knock it. The body brush is also used to brush its mane and tail. If you comb its mane with a mane comb, do it carefully, as the hairs will break very easily.

Clean its eyes, nostrils and dock with a damp sponge.

Brush around and under its hooves with hoof oil.

Wipe it all over with a clean cloth to make its coat gleam; as a finishing touch, smooth down its mane and tail with a damp brush.

Hoof pick

Dandy brush

Body brush

Metal currycomb

Rubber currycomb

Mane comb

Hoof oil and brush

Sponge and bucket

Cloth

Shoeing

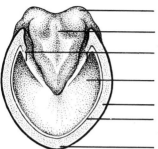

Parts of the hoof

Heel – Back of hoof

Frog – Acts as a cushion and pumps blood through the foot

Bars – Where the wall turns in

Sole – Guards the foot, but can become bruised

Wall – Naillike, no feeling

White line – Between feeling and nonfeeling parts of hoof

Toe – Front of hoof

Most working horses and ponies need to wear metal horseshoes, to keep their feet from getting worn down. Shoes also keep the hoof from becoming cracked, bruised or out of shape.

If your pony works a lot, it will need new shoes every six weeks. In that time, the shoes may wear smooth, and the pony's feet will grow out of them.

Horseshoes must be made to fit properly. The blacksmith (or farrier) takes the old shoe off first. Then he trims down the wall of the hoof, and fits a new shoe. The shoe will fit better if it is hot and pliable. The shoe is nailed to the wall of the hoof where it won't hurt the pony. Finally, the blacksmith files the surface of the shoe smooth.

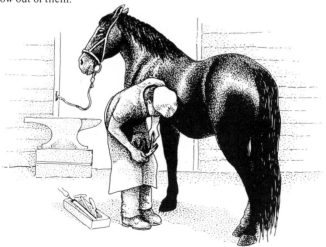

Riding

A horse has to be carefully prepared before it is ready to be ridden. This is known as "breaking" and "schooling". The horse has to get used to having a rider on its back, and must learn to obey commands. A horse can be broken for riding when it is three years old, and will have an active life until it is 20, if well cared for. (Horses normally live for 25 to 30 years.)

A rider has just as much to learn as a horse does. He must learn to sit so that the horse is well-balanced and can move freely. He must also learn to give the horse signals it can understand.

If you want to learn to ride, find a riding school that is approved, so you can be sure your teacher is a

good one. You should be given a quiet, well-schooled horse or pony to begin on.

These are the aids a rider uses to control his horse:

Hands – These hold the reins which control the bit. The bit lies on a sensitive part of the horse's jaw, so you must keep a steady but gentle contact with the bit. Use your hands to slow your horse down, and to turn it to the right or left.

Legs – Use your lower leg and heel to make your horse move forward, and turn properly (bending its spine). Your legs should be close to the horse's body. Your heels should be pushed down. If the horse moves suddenly, try to keep your balance and keep your body relaxed.

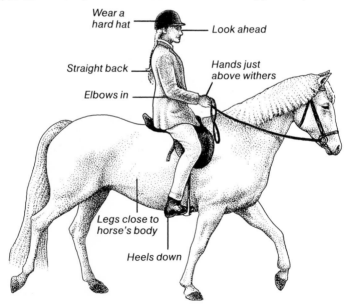

Wear a hard hat

Look ahead

Straight back

Hands just above withers

Elbows in

Legs close to horse's body

Heels down

Body – Body weight can be used to drive the horse forward. If you want to slow down, let your weight sink into the saddle. The horse will easily keep its balance if your seat is proper. The legs and reins are all that is needed to make the horse change direction.

Voice – Horses have very sharp hearing, and can learn to recognize many sounds. To encourage your horse to move forward if it hesitates, click your tongue. A slow, quiet "Whoa . . . ", used with the proper seat and rein movement, will slow it down. Never scream or shout near a horse. This will frighten it and it may bolt.

Tack

Good tack (saddles and bridles) is very important. A plain snaffle bridle is best for most ponies. Fit the bridle carefully; ask someone to help you adjust it to fit your pony if you aren't sure how to do it.

For ordinary riding, a general purpose saddle is best. The saddle sits on the pony's back, just behind the withers; it should be well clear of the pony's spine at all times.

Tack is made of leather. You should clean your tack every time you use it, to prevent it becoming hard, and cracking. Clean it with a damp sponge first, then saddle soap it to keep it soft.

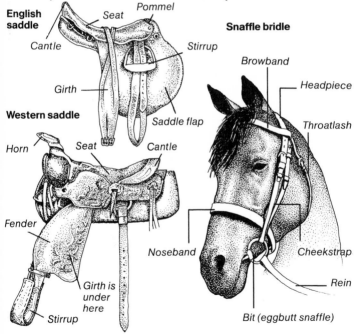

English saddle
Seat
Pommel
Cantle
Stirrup
Girth
Saddle flap

Western saddle
Horn
Seat
Cantle
Fender
Girth is under here
Stirrup

Snaffle bridle
Browband
Headpiece
Throatlash
Noseband
Cheekstrap
Rein
Bit (eggbutt snaffle)

Glossary

All-rounder – horse or pony that is good at different things, like jumping, hunting and gymkhana games.

Cob – short, stocky horse (not more than 15.3 hh). Quiet and well-behaved.

Colt – male horse up to three years old.

Dressage – the training of a horse. It includes breaking and basic schooling, as well as the more advanced, precision movements that are performed by well-schooled, obedient horses.

Event horse – used in horse trials, which include dressage, show jumping and cross-country riding.

Filly – female horse up to three years old.

Flat racing – racing over short courses without jumps.

Foal – male or female horse up to one year old.

Gelding – male horse that has been de-sexed.

Gymkhana – show where mounted games and races (eg. barrel-racing and keyhole) are held.

Hack – well-behaved, well-schooled riding horse of light build. Some women ride hacks side-saddle.

Hunter – horse that can gallop cross-country and jump well. It must be strong and very fit.

Hurdler – horse that races and jumps hurdles, usually over courses about two and a half miles long.

Mare – female horse more than three years old.

Point-to-point – amateur jumping races. They used to be run from one church steeple (point) to the next.

School master – old, well-behaved,

In this gymkhana race, riders lose marks if they spill water

well-schooled horse or pony. Safe and reliable for people learning to ride.

Show jumping – jumping competitions.

Show horse/pony – competes at shows in various classes, like "Working Hunter" or "Children's Riding Pony". Judged on its appearance, schooling and suitability for the class entered.

Stallion – male horse more than three years old. Usually kept only for breeding.

Steeplechase – race run over fences on courses which are about five miles long.

Trotter – horse or pony that races in harness; it may either trot or "pace" (move the fore and hind legs on each side together).

Hunter

Mare and foal

Riding vacations

There are various kinds of riding vacations; some teach special skills, such as show jumping or dressage, and others cater for people who just want to go horseback riding in the country. Before you go on one, you should have several riding lessons. You can find out about riding vacations by looking through pony and horse magazines and the travel section of a large newspaper, or by visiting a travel agency.

There are many riding schools throughout North America that offer programs lasting from 3 months to two years (and sometimes longer). The students usually live at the school and pay room and board as well as tuition. Most of these schools cover riding, training and stable management. It is a good idea to visit the school first to make certain that it has a high standard. If you are interested in a Bachelor of Science degree some colleges and universities now offer programs in equine (horse) science.

Horseback riding in the country

You don't need a great deal of experience if you want to vacation at a dude ranch or camp. You will be given a horse (or pony) to ride and you may have to feed and groom it yourself. Some ranches or camps give riding instructions. Some offer whole- or half-day trips and occasionally overnight pack trips as well.

Dude ranch or camp

Useful addresses

American Driving Society, 339 Warburton Avenue, Hastings-on-Hudson, NY 10706.

National Steeplechase and Hunt, P.O. Box 308, Elmont, NY 11003.

U.S. Combined Training Association, 1 Winthrop Square, Boston, MA 02110.

National Horse and Pony Youth Activities Council, 929 South Fourth Street, Louisville, KY 40203.

Professional Rodeo Cowboys Association, 2929 West 19th Avenue, Denver, CO 80204.

United States Pony Clubs, 303 South High Street, West Chester, PA 19380.

National 4-H Service Committee, 150 North Wacker Drive, Chicago, IL 60606.

American Horse Shows Association, 598 Madison Avenue, New York, NY 10022.

Canadian Equestrian Federation, 333 River Road, Ottawa, Ontario KIL 8B9.

Books to read

The Classic World of Horses. Robert Magee (Arco Publishing Co.). An illustrated reference covering several aspects of the sport.

Riding from A to Z. Peter Churchill (Taplinger Publishing Co.). A solid, practical horseman's guide.

Showing and Ringcraft Explained. Ronnie Mutch (Arco Publishing Co.). An excellent practical manual. Well illustrated.

Western Horse Behavior and Training. Robert W. Miller (Double-day and Co., Inc.). A detailed reference for training the western horse.

The Light Horse Breeds. John W. Patten (A.S. Barnes & Co., Inc.). An informative and historical reference.

The Horse Owner's Handbook. Lloyd S. McKibbin, D.V.M. (W.B. Saunders Co.). An excellent reference book about injuries and illnesses in the horse. Well illustrated.

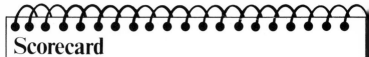

Scorecard

The horses and ponies on this score-card are arranged in alphabetical order. When you see one, write down the date in the blank space next to each name and circle your score. You can add up your score after a day at a horse show, for instance.

Akhal-Teke	25		Dartmoor	15	
American Saddlebred	5		Don	25	
Andalusian	15		Dutch Draft	20	
Anglo-Arab	10		Exmoor	15	
Anglo-Norman	20		Falabella	20	
Appaloosa	5		Fell	20	
Arab (any type)	5		Finnish	20	
Ardennes	20		Fjord	20	
Auxois	25		Fredericksborg	25	
Avelignese	25		Friesian	25	
Barb	25		Gelderlander	20	
Boulonnais	25		Gotland	25	
Breton	20		Groningen	25	
Budyonny	25		Gudbrandsaal	25	
Carmargue	20		Hackney	5	
Caspian	25		Haflinger	15	
Cleveland Bay	15		Hanoverian	15	
Clydesdale	10		Highland	15	
Connemara	5		Holstein	10	
Criollo	25		Huçul	25	
Dales	15		Icelandic	20	

Irish Draft	15		Shire	10	
Jutland	25		Standardbred	5	
Karabair	25		Suffolk Punch	20	
Kazakh	25		Tarpan	25	
Kladruber	25		Tennessee Walking Horse	5	
Knabstrup	25		Thoroughbred	5	
Kustanair	25		Trait du Nord	25	
Lipizzaner	10		Trakehner	15	
Lusitano	25		Turkoman	25	
Morgan	5		Vladimir	25	
New Forest	20		Waler	25	
Nonius	25		Welsh Cob	5	
Oldenburger	20		Welsh Mountain	15	
Orlov Trotter	25		Wielkopolski	25	
Palomino	5				
Paso Fino	10				
Percheron	10				
Pinto	5				
Pinzgauer Noriker	25				
Pony of the Americas	5				
Przewalski	20				
Quarter Horse	5				
Sable Island	25				
Schleswig	20				
Shetland	5				

Index